BEAUTIFUL

JIM BRICKMAN, JACK KUGELL
and JAMIE JONES

Slow ballad (♩ = 60)

25324

© 2002 UNIVERSAL TUNES, a Division of SONGS OF UNIVERSAL, INC., BRICKMAN SONGS,
EMI APRIL MUSIC INC., DOXIE MUSIC, MIMI'S MUSIC MAN PRODUCTIONS and DAYSPRING MUSIC, INC.
All Rights for BRICKMAN SONGS Controlled and Administered by UNIVERSAL TUNES, A Division of SONGS OF UNIVERSAL, INC.
All Rights for DOXIE MUSIC Controlled and Administered by EMI APRIL MUSIC INC.
All Rights for MIMI'S MUSIC MAN PRODUCTIONS Controlled and Administered by DAYSPRING MUSIC, INC.
All Rights Reserved

BECAUSE OF YOU

Words and Music by
KELLY CLARKSON, BEN MOODY
and DAVID HODGES

Moderately slow (♩ = 72)

© 2004 Smelly Songs, SmellsLikeMetal Publishing and Dwight Frye Music, Inc.
All Rights for SmellsLikeMetal Publishing Administered by Dwight Frye Music, Inc. (BMI)
All Rights Reserved

2005 2006 Greatest Pop Hits

This book features a specially designed Violin arrangement for the young Violinist. Each arrangement features a carefully crafted part complete with bowings, articulations, and keys well suited for the Level 2-3 player.

This book is also part of an instrumental series written for Flute, Clarinet, Alto Sax, Tenor Sax, Trumpet, and Trombone. Due to level considerations regarding keys and instrument ranges, the arrangements in the wind instrument series are not compatible with those in this violin book.

© 2006 ALFRED PUBLISHING CO., INC.
All Rights Reserved

Any duplication, adaptation or arrangement of the compositions
contained in this collection requires the written consent of the Publisher.
No part of this book may be photocopied or reproduced in any way without permission.
Unauthorized uses are an infringement of the U.S. Copyright Act and are punishable by law.

Contents

Chorus:

BELIEVER

Moderately slow ballad (♩ = 84)

Words and Music by
will.i.am and John Legend

© 2005 United Lion Music, Inc., Cherry Lane Music Publishing Company, obo itself
and Cherry River Music Co., will.i.am music, inc. and John Legend Publishing
All Rights Reserved

25324

EMOTIONAL

Words and Music by
ANDREAS CARLSSON,
DESMOND CHILD and CHRIS BRAIDE

25324

© 2004 WB MUSIC CORP., ANDREAS CARLSSON PUBLISHING AB, DESTON SONGS, LLC, DESMOBILE, INC. and VISIBLE MUSIC LTD.
All Rights for itself, ANDREAS CARLSSON PUBLISHING AB, DESTON SONGS, LLC and DESMOBILE, INC. Administered by WB MUSIC CORP.
All Rights for VISIBLE MUSIC LTD. Administered by WARNER/CHAPPELL MUSIC LTD.
All Rights Reserved

BOULEVARD OF BROKEN DREAMS

Words by BILLIE JOE
Music by GREEN DAY

Moderate rock (♩ = 86)

Verses 1 & 2:

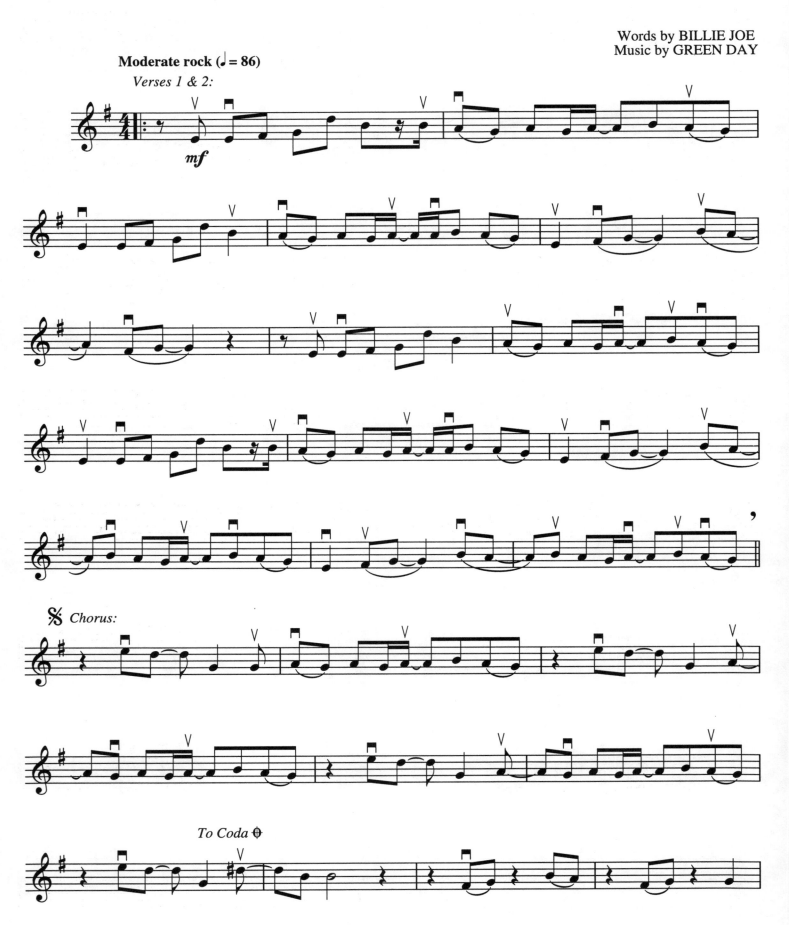

To Coda ⊕

© 2004 WB Music Corp. (ASCAP) and Green Daze Music (ASCAP)
All Rights Administered by WB Music Corp.
All Rights Reserved

BREAKAWAY

Words and Music by
MATTHEW GERRARD, AVRIL LAVIGNE
and BRIDGET BENENATE

© 2004 WB Music Corp., G Matt Music, Almo Music Corp., Avril Lavigne Publishing Ltd.,
Music of Windswept, Blotter Music and Friends Of Seagulls Music
All Rights for G Matt Music Administered by WB Music Corp.
All Rights for Avril Lavigne Publishing Ltd. Administered by Almo Music Corp.
All Rights Reserved

To Coda ⊕

Bridge:

mf

D.S. 𝄋 al Coda

⊕
Coda

p

EVERYTHING BURNS

Words and Music by
BEN MOODY

Moderately slow (♩ = 96)

Verse 1:

Chorus:

© 2005 SMELLSLIKEMETAL PUBLISHING and DWIGHT FRYE MUSIC, INC. (BMI)
All Rights Administered by DWIGHT FRYE MUSIC, INC. (BMI)
All Rights Reserved

Verse 2:

Chorus:

GOOD IS GOOD

Words and Music by
SHERYL CROW and JEFF TROTT

© 2005 WARNER-TAMERLANE PUBLISHING CORP., OLD CROW MUSIC and CYRILLIC SOUP
All Rights on behalf of itself and OLD CROW MUSIC Administered by WARNER-TAMERLANE PUBLISHING CORP.
All Rights for CYRILLIC SOUP Administered by WIXEN MUSIC PUBLISHING INC.
All Rights Reserved

I'M FEELING YOU

Words and Music by
JOHN SHANKS,
MICHELLE BRANCH
and KARA DIOGUARDI

© 2004 WB MUSIC CORP., DYLAN JACKSON MUSIC, WARNER-TAMERLANE PUBLISHING CORP.,
I'M STILL WITH THE BAND MUSIC and K'STUFF PUBLISHING
All Rights on behalf of itself and DYLAN JACKSON MUSIC Administered by WB MUSIC CORP.
All Rights on behalf of itself and I'M STILL WITH THE BAND MUSIC Administered by WARNER-TAMERLANE PUBLISHING CORP.
All Rights Reserved

25324

HUNG UP

Words and Music by
MADONNA, STUART PRICE,
BENNY ANDERSSON and BJÖRN ULVAEUS

© 2005 WEBO GIRL PUBLISHING, INC. and DARKDANCER LTD.
All Rights for WEBO GIRL PUBLISHING, INC. Administered by WB MUSIC CORP.
All Rights for DARKDANCER LTD. in the U.S.A. Administered by WB MUSIC CORP.
This song contains samples from "GIMME! GIMME! GIMME! (A MAN AFTER MIDNIGHT)"
Words and Music by BENNY ANDERSSON and BJÖRN ULVAEUS, © UNION SONGS MUSIKFORLAG AB (STIM)
All Rights Reserved

INSIDE YOUR HEAVEN

Words and Music by
ANDREAS CARLSSON, PER NYLEN
and SAVAN KOTECHA

Inside Your Heaven - 2 - 1
25324

© 2005 WB MUSIC CORP., ANDREAS CARLSSON PUBLISHING AB,
UNIVERSAL MUSIC PUBLISHING AB and OH SUKI MUSIC
All Rights for itself and ANDREAS CARLSSON PUBLISHING AB Administered by WB MUSIC CORP.
All Rights Reserved

LIKE WE NEVER LOVED AT ALL

Words and Music by
JOHN RICH, VICKY McGEHEE
and SCOTT SACKS

© 2005 WB MUSIC CORP., WARNER-TAMERLANE PUBLISHING CORP. and
SCOTSAXSONGS, Administered by PEN MUSIC GROUP
All Rights Reserved

Like We Never Loved At All - 2 - 2
25324

LOST WITHOUT YOU

Words and Music by
MATTHEW GERRARD and
BRIDGET BENENATE

25324
© 2003 WB MUSIC CORP., G MATT MUSIC, WINDSWEPT PACIFIC MUSIC, BLOTTER MUSIC and FRIENDS OF SEAGULLS MUSIC PUBLISHING
All Rights on behalf of itself and G MATT MUSIC Administered by WB MUSIC CORP.
All Rights on behalf of itself, BLOTTER MUSIC and FRIENDS OF SEAGULLS MUSIC PUBLISHING Administered by WINDSWEPT PACIFIC MUSIC
All Rights Reserved

MAGIC WORKS

By JARVIS COCKER

© 2005 WARNER-OLIVE MUSIC, LLC and WARNER CHAPPELL MUSIC LTD.
All Rights Administered by WB MUSIC CORP.
All Rights Reserved

NO MORE CLOUDY DAYS

Words and Music by
GLENN FREY

© 2005 RED CLOUD MUSIC (BMI)
All Print Rights Administered by WARNER-TAMERLANE PUBLISHING CORP.
All Rights Reserved

STICKWITU

Words and Music by
FRANNE GOLDE, KASIA LIVINGSTON
and ROBERT PALMER

© 2005 FRANNE GEE MUSIC, DAD'S DREAMER MUSIC, PEERMUSIC LTD. and PARCHI MUSIC
All Rights for FRANNE GEE MUSIC Administered by WARNER-TAMERLANE PUBLISHING CORP.
All Rights Reserved

OVER

Words and Music by
JOHN SHANKS, KARA DIOGUARDI
and LINDSAY LOHAN

Over - 2 - 1
25324

© 2004 WB MUSIC CORP., JOHN SHANKS MUSIC, K'STUFF PUBLISHING and CROSSHEART LLC
All Rights for itself and JOHN SHANKS MUSIC Administered by WB MUSIC CORP.
All Rights Reserved

PHOTOGRAPH

Lyrics by CHAD KROEGER
Music by NICKELBACK

(Play cue note 2nd time)

Chorus:

© 2005 WARNER-TAMERLANE PUBLISHING CORP., ARM YOUR DILLO PUBLISHING, INC.,
ZERO-G MUSIC INC. and BLACK DIESEL MUSIC INC.
All Rights Administered by WARNER-TAMERLANE PUBLISHING CORP.
All Rights Reserved

READY TO FLY

Words and Music by
RICHARD MARX

© 2002 Chi-Boy Music (ASCAP)
All Rights Reserved

STRANGER IN A STRANGE LAND

Words and Music by
BARRY GIBB, ASHLEY GIBB
and STEPHEN GIBB

© 2005 CROMPTON SONGS, GEE SON SONGS and TUNE-O-MATIC SONGS
All Rights Administered by WARNER-TAMERLANE PUBLISHING CORP.
All Rights Reserved

UNTITLED
(How Can This Happen to Me?)

Words and Music by
SIMPLE PLAN

Moderately slow ($\quad$ = 92)

legato Verse 1:

%8 *Chorus:*

mf - f

To Coda ⊕

Untitled - 2 - 1
25324

© 2004 WB MUSIC CORP., WET WHEELIE MUSIC and HIGH-MAINTENANCE MUSIC
All Rights Administered by WB MUSIC CORP.
All Rights Reserved

Verse 2:

WAKE ME UP WHEN SEPTEMBER ENDS

Words by BILLIE JOE
Music by GREEN DAY

© 2004 WB Music Corp. (ASCAP) and Green Daze Music (ASCAP)
All Rights Administered by WB Music Corp.
All Rights Reserved

WHEN YOU TELL ME THAT YOU LOVE ME

Words and Music by
ALBERT HAMMOND and JOHN BETTIS

When You Tell Me That You Love Me - 2 - 1
25324

© 1991 JOHN BETTIS MUSIC and ALBERT HAMMOND MUSIC
All Rights for JOHN BETTIS MUSIC Administered by WB MUSIC CORP.
All Rights for ALBERT HAMMOND MUSIC Administered by
WINDSWEPT PACIFIC ENTERTAINMENT CO. d/b/a LONGITUDE MUSIC
All Rights Reserved

WINDOW TO MY HEART

Words and Music by
JON SECADA and
MIGUEL MOREJON

© 2005 Foreign Imported Productions & Publishing, Inc. (BMI)
International Rights Secured
All Rights Reserved

Bridge:

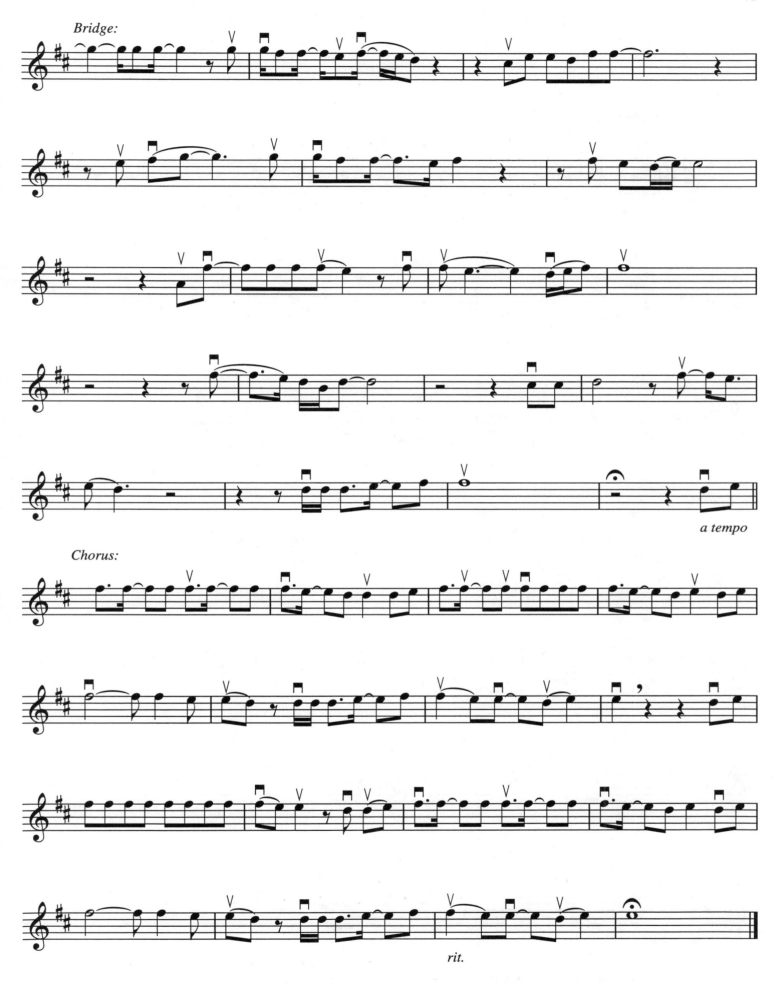

a tempo

Chorus:

rit.

YOU AND ME

Words and Music by
JUDE COLE and JASON WADE

© 2005 WARNER-TAMERLANE PUBLISHING CORP., JUDE COLE MUSIC, G. CHILLS MUSIC and DIMENSIONAL SONGS OF THE KNOLL
All Rights on behalf of itself and JUDE COLE MUSIC Administered by WARNER-TAMERLANE PUBLISHING CORP.
All Rights Reserved

Bridge:

Chorus:

mp